LOVING ME

I0459166

LOVING ME

THE HIDDEN AGENDA OF SELF-ESTEEM

RICK THOMAS

LOVING ME:
The Hidden Agenda of Self-esteem

ISBN 978-1-966741-05-3

Rick Thomas

© 2025 Life Over Coffee

Unless otherwise noted, all Scripture references herein are from the English Standard Version, copyright © 2001 by Crossway, Inc. Used by permission. All rights reserved.

No part of this publication may be reproduced, stored in a retrieval system, or transmitted in any form or by any means without the express written permission of Life Over Coffee.

Edited by Sarah Hayhurst

Life Over Coffee
8595 Pelham Rd Ste 400 #406,
Greenville, SC 29615
LifeOverCoffee.com

Dedication

To those who struggle with living in the freedom of
the Imago Dei, hoping to break away from the self-
esteem agenda. I trust this book will bring the hope
and help you need to benefit from the fullness of what
it means to be free in Christ alone as you love God
and others as yourself.

.

For additional resources, visit
lifeovercoffee.com

Table of Contents

Introduction

Mable walked into the woods one day, doused herself with gasoline, and set herself on fire. The newspapers said she suffered from low self-esteem. They were wrong. Regrettably, Mable was preoccupied with herself. She could not stop thinking about herself, her problems, those who mocked her, put her down, alienated her, and a myriad of other everyday disappointments from family and friends. Her thoughts in the fortress of her mind would not release her from a self-centered preoccupation that led her into the woods, the only path she knew that would break the mental stronghold and soul noise consuming her.

End of the Road

Mable had an extremely high view of herself, an ideal of what she wished to be. In her twisted and tormented mind, she could not become that person. Rather than resting in the Imago Dei (image of God), she wanted acceptance, respect, and love from the culture (Genesis 1:27). Mable did not know God; the only person she could compare herself to was the ideal defined by her culture, leaving her with no escape from a miserable life. She could not rise to what she believed was everyone's expectations, and all their mocking and alienation did not help. Mable accepted her fate and destroyed the person she despised.

Mable's story is true. I knew her. I liked her because she

was like me: quiet, reserved, and not part of the popular set. Though she was different from those who were outgoing, she was also the same as them. She is a snapshot of everyone. Since the fall of Adam, self-consumption has been a dominant aspect of our thought lives. Individualism, over-evaluation, and self-preoccupation are the Adamic trifecta that send the mind to dark places. When thinking about ourselves, personal loyalty is natural and expected, though there is an incredible downside.

Sin is always crouching at the door of our hearts, ready to push us further than we want to go. Mable's admiration for herself had no holy parameters, so sin took her further than she intended to go and required more than she wanted to pay. She did not know any other way out of her mind (Philippians 2:3–4; John 14:6). The end of the road for the person drowning with accelerated self-thoughts is suicide. How could it be otherwise? The more she reflected on herself, the more dissatisfied she became with what she saw. Her hopelessness grew with each despairing look, and finally, the only solution was to remove the problem. She set herself on fire.

From Adam, We Came

To esteem yourself outside the parameters of the Imago Dei is to have an elevated view of yourself the way the culture does. Words like respect, admiration, value, and appreciation fit within the domain of these esteemers; they become some of their idols. Of course, if our estimation of ourselves cannot rise to that lofty place, then the esteemer will always wrestle with self-condemning thought-fortresses or what Paul called strongholds (2 Corinthians 10:3–6). The biblical appeal is to assume your value from an Imago Dei presupposition, which changes our thoughts directionally—away from ourselves and toward God and others. There is no need to spend our days thinking about ourselves if we're resting and secure in the reality that God created us in His image. Our view of ourselves does not need realignment once the Bible calibrates our thinking.

Every Christian knows and rests in their worth in God, so to spend time focusing on themselves is redundant, inward, and misguided. If you are a believer who struggles with worth, the answer is not thinking more about yourself but thinking more about Christ in you and the Father who created you in His image (Genesis 1:27; Psalm 139:14). We will never find hope in ourselves. If Adam had thought more about God than himself, he would not have attempted to elevate himself into an ideological space that could never satisfy, as he soon learned (Genesis 3:6–12). Satan was determined to turn Adam into himself by suggesting that God was a liar—there is a better world than what God offered, a sales pitch that deceived Mable too.

You can read the entire sordid story of how Adam went from God-centered to self-centered in Genesis 3:6–12. Adam exchanged the truth of God for a lie and began to worship himself more than his Creator (Romans 1:25). Once Adam made his first move away from God, he had to double down by insulating himself with fig leaves. One wrong decision leads to another—ad infinitum. Adam was feeling the effects of his movements, and rather than running back to God, he covered his shame while scurrying from the garden, lied about what was going on, and threw Eve under the bus. Adamic people caught in the trap of esteeming themselves more than God wrestle with Adam's characteristics.

- They will struggle with shame.
- They will struggle with fear.
- They will not find rest in the truths of the Imago Dei.
- They will not want God poking around their lives.
- They will practice deceit to hide the truth about themselves.
- They will blame their problems on others.

Self-esteem's Cure

The culture will tell a person like Mable they need to esteem themselves more. The problem with turning yourself onto yourself to think better about yourself has never been the answer. Self-centeredness binds the soul until the weight of our thoughts buries us in a hole of hopelessness. The cure for self-esteem is to think of ourselves less while considering God and others more. If we continue to give our minds over to thoughts about ourselves, we will end up like Adam with complicated views and distorted relationships. The message of the gospel is always counter to unregenerate, human wisdom.

For the foolishness of God is wiser than men, and the weakness of God is stronger than men.
(1 Corinthians 1:25)

What looks like wisdom and strength from the culture's perspective is not, and what seems like foolishness and weakness of God is not. Adam should have let go of what was best for him, according to Satan, and grabbed hold of what was best from God. Jesus said we could sum up all the Old Testament's 600 (plus) laws in four words— love God, love others. It's the best advice we'll ever receive if we want to be whole (Matthew 22:36–40). The fullest and happiest people you'll ever meet are those who find no greater joy than to give their lives to others. The most miserable and angry people you'll ever meet cannot stop thinking about themselves as they work to fill the insatiable hole in their souls, often comparing themselves to others.

Not that we dare to classify or compare ourselves with some of those who are commending themselves. But when they measure themselves by one another and compare themselves with one another, they are without understanding.

(2 Corinthians 10:12)

Mable had an ideal of herself that she esteemed more than anything else. That version was a vision of what she wanted to be. Mable loved that ideal person as she compared it to whom she was. She always came up short, as defined and determined by the culture's view of wholeness. According to Paul, Mable was without understanding, a harsh response, but not nearly as awful as the path she chose. According to the culture, she had low self-esteem. In the end, Mable hated the person she was; she loved her ideological view of herself. Her esteem of the person she could not be was on steroids, which could only end with self-destruction.

Call to Action

Suicide was a last-ditch effort to end the misery and find restorative hope through those drastic means. She was hopelessly stuck on herself. It sounds unsympathetic, but it would have been the path to a new destination. Wholeness comes through Christ alone (Colossians 1:28). God makes us complete, the first step that releases us from self-preoccupation and self-consumption. Complete people pursue God and others more than themselves. Loving God and others will not deplete anyone. It will fill us with more of God's character and attributes, releasing us for more of His empowering favor (James 4:6).

1. What is the subtle and entrapping lie of high self-esteem?
2. Satan did not mention to Adam or Mable that if they tried to become like a god, it would not end well for them (Proverbs 14:12). Have you listened to those lies? If so, perhaps sharing with a friend what the pathway is like when we walk away from God.
3. Have you been shaped to think poorly of yourself? How have familial or cultural perspectives, words, and actions shaped you adversely?
4. Why is the path to freedom a steady stream of thinking less about yourself and more about God and others?
5. Will you share how the two great commandments release you from self-consumption with a friend?
6. How would you help a person like Mable?

1

The Fallacy and Futility

Self-esteem teaching has been around for a long time. It's one of the central planks of the culture's gospel, which is their attempt to feel better about themselves. They, like us, realize they need help. As ambassadors for Christ, we must know how to engage cultural friends, to help them while keeping an eye on their version of psychology to ensure that we don't fall for their traps. The fallacy and futility of the self-esteem gospel are everywhere, so learning to debunk it with competence, courage, and compassion is every believer's responsibility.

The Culture's View

Without biblical filters, it's easy to take the world's ways for a spin, especially if the Christian is not adept at applying God's Word personally or practically—what we call biblical psychology (psyche-logos), which means studying the soul. For the Christian, the Bible (2 Timothy 3:16) applied practically and personally to our souls (Genesis 2:7) is the purest form of psychology. A lack of practical application of God's Word opens the way for the culture to peddle its view of psychology. The temptation is easier than one might think. Their way does not require the hard work of connecting the Bible to our personal lives, and who doesn't like easy?

The Bible does not teach self-esteem, which should be the most significant red flag of all. However, the silence of the Bible on this post-modern doctrine does not deter the Christian self-esteem advocate from trumpeting this dangerous doctrine within the church. God went to great lengths to free us from spending so much time thinking about ourselves. He clearly communicated our badness so that when we look at ourselves, we should sense hopelessness and a pinch of motivation to turn our gaze toward Him. From God's perspective, human success and personal wholeness happen when we master those five syllables, which has a distinct upward and outward focus.

A Better Way

The retort, from self-esteem advocates, says esteeming yourself is the opposite of self-loathing. It is. Sort of. But before I refute their doctrine, it might be helpful to understand why the world is groping for the walls like blind creatures, creating a doctrine that cannot hold water. Mainly, they need something besides biblical psychology because they reject God's Word. It's not as though they can sit in the corner with a dunce cap on. They have to devise a worldview and methodology to understand the soul. Hence, self-esteem fits the bill perfectly because it keeps the focus on the individual. The unwitting design of self-esteem and self-loathing is to ensure the capturing and incarcerating of the soul in a hermetically sealed universe of self.

The Bible presents a better way to think about ourselves. It's called made in the image of God—the Imago Dei (Genesis 1:27), a profound way to think about God and His creation. Self-esteem perpetuates self-focus while the Imago Dei turns our thoughts upward and outward, encompassing our Creator and all humanity. As we turn our sight lines from ourselves toward God, we begin to see the world He made through His eyes rather than ours. It is stunning to the Christian that the Lord would set us apart from the rest of His creative order, and out of that humble God-awareness of what He did grows respect for what He created. We don't value ourselves or others less, but we see the miraculous blessedness of the Imago Dei, which circumvents any desire for self-loathing and accentuates our admiration and respect for God and others.

Presuppositions and Words

Self-esteem does not enhance our thoughts about God and others to that degree because the culture word smithers and label makers did not factor God and His Word into their psychology. Of course, none of this would matter if Christians were less in tune with the culture while more dialed into God's Word. We have a penchant for hijacking their words and ways and shoehorning them into our understanding of biblical psychology, even twisting their language to fit our fads. Theologian John Piper made this mistake when he tried to reinvent the word hedonism by reframing it as Christian hedonism. He instilled unnecessary tension in the believer's mind. Thankfully, it only caught on for a season.

Pulling an unnecessary word from the culture—hedonism or self-esteem—and inserting it into the Christian's vocabulary is not helpful. The Bible has given us all we need to think rightly about God, ourselves, and others. Words have presuppositions—interpretive lens, and if a word has such a firm hold on the mind, i.e., hedonism, trying to make it mean something nobody ever expected is not wise. Sometimes, we can outsmart ourselves to our detriment. I'm not suggesting we should refrain from all everyday human language. Perhaps an example of a woman who went through horrible abuse from her father would be helpful.

Later in life, she became a Christian, and her friends introduced her to God the Father. She already knew what a father was, so when they told her about her new heavenly Father, she struggled to relate well with Him. The solution for her is not to refrain from using the everyday word, father, but to learn and apply the differences between an abusive father and a loving one. We live in the world; we use their language when appropriate, but when it comes to soul care, biblical precision is our call, and there is some language that we should never smuggle into how we speak about transformation. Self-esteem would be one of those terms.

Choose Wise Battles

Every situation requires wisdom. With our abused friend, we would carefully and compassionately redefine the word father for her. Paul did this for his Jewish friends who were new to Christianity, as seen in 1 Corinthians 8:1–13. They were struggling with what to do with the meat their new brothers and sisters were eating. Sometimes, we have no choice but to redefine a word—father—or an idea— meat—because it confuses the person due to their former associations with that word or concept (1 Corinthians 8:7; Ephesians 4:22). However, self-esteem should not be part of a Christian's vocabulary.

When you meet a Christian whom the culture has indoctrinated, you can show them a new and better way to understand the soul. You can do this without becoming the word police. I rarely say anything about a person's use of secular words like self-esteem. A lousy word is not my cue to go on the offensive by telling them it's a bad word. The word is not their biggest problem, and we don't want to exacerbate their fear of man by mandating that they use the proper word. Using biblical methodologies, we can compassionately and patiently teach them the truth to help them toward transformation. Later, we can clean up their vocab. Too many biblical counselors shoot at people like targets because of their poor word choices while missing the opportunity to care for them.

Path To Freedom

Made in the image of God is the correct language. For starters, it teaches biblical respect for every person—saved or lost. When a person understands the value of the person because of who created them, it becomes a challenge to hate themselves. We cannot hate ourselves or others when the Imago Dei correctly calibrates and aligns our thinking. Perhaps it would help to take a self-assessment to see how the Imago Dei manages your thoughts, creating an attitude toward others, especially those with whom you disagree. Here are a few sample questions to assess yourself.

- Is there someone you are sinfully angry with currently, and you refuse to repent to them, though you know you should?
- Do you view yourself as better than a [cultural] person?
- Do you feel superior to people not of your cultural demographic?
- Do you self-harm?
- Are you characterized as self-critical?

If you answered yes to any of these questions, your understanding and practice of the Imago Dei needs recalibrating. For the record, the self-esteem doctrine will not teach you how to answer no to any of these questions, except for the last one, which is the point of self-esteem: to love yourself more than others. Some will argue that you must love yourself before you can love others. Of course, they will not give you any Scripture to support that idea, though they try to parachute their perspective into Matthew 22:36–40. It's a weird argument that does not consider what I just said about the Imago Dei. If you dislike yourself (or anyone else), the solution is not better self-esteem but a better understanding of what it means for God to make you in His image. You see this idea in James 3:9–10:

> With it [the tongue] we bless our Lord and Father, and with it we curse people who are made in the likeness [image] of God. From the same mouth come blessing and cursing. My brothers, these things ought not to be so.

If someone has harassed you to the point where you are painfully insecure, or you're tempted to self-loathing, it would be a mistake to turn your focus onto yourself, as though learning to love yourself is the cure. Learning to love God is your cure. Paul said it this way,

> And we all, with unveiled face, beholding the glory of the Lord, are being transformed into the same image from one degree of glory to another. For this comes from the Lord who is the Spirit.
>
> (2 Corinthians 3:18)

Repair the Broken

Learning, loving, adoring, and worshiping God is the path to freedom. And that's just the beginning of the good news. Being made in the image of God puts us on the right path to how we must think about ourselves, but it's not the end of our journey to wholeness. We, like all humanity, are under the unrelenting challenges of total depravity—a concept that means there is nothing about us that is unaffected by sin, physically and spiritually. This teaching is one more reason to run from self-esteem: nothing in us is exempt from the marring of sin, including our thoughts about ourselves. Looking into the inner darkness of a depraved soul draws the searcher deeper into the cave of hopelessness.

Paul said we have become worthless (Romans 3:12). No amount of secular, humanistic, psychological engineering can fix our problem with God and each other. We are thoroughly corrupted from the inside out. Sin has decimated the core of our very being. Because our culture denies God, they have no choice but to create a self-focused doctrine like self-esteem. From there, they teach innate human goodness and an ability to do all things "through themselves who strengthens themselves" psychological worldview. God teaches total depravity, how we're a dime of dozen, recyclable containers who will never save ourselves from ourselves (2 Corinthians 1:8–9, 4:7).

The wealthiest and most famous people in our culture have died while still chasing the holy grail of self-esteem. Many finished their journeys as empty as when they began (Job 1:21; Ecclesiastes 1:8). Pursuing self-esteem will drive the soul into the ground. It's an insatiable pursuit of self-worth sought outside the transforming power of Christ. Our worth will come as Christ fills us with His righteousness. We crucify ourselves through the incremental process of putting away our former manner of life, with all its self-esteem, and putting on a new kind of person radically different from who we were (Ephesians 4:24). That new person is like God. The more Christlike we become, the more we will experience wholeness (Colossians 1:28).

> I have been crucified with Christ. It is no longer I who live, but Christ who lives in me. And the life I now live in the flesh I live by faith in the Son of God, who loved me and gave himself for me.
>
> (Galatians 2:20)

Thinking Less

Put off your old self, which belongs to your former manner of life and is corrupt through deceitful desires, and to be renewed in the spirit of your minds, and to put on the new self, created after the likeness of God in true righteousness and holiness.

(Ephesians 4:22–24)

Tim Keller had the best quote about self-esteem when he said, "The essence of gospel-humility is not thinking more of myself or thinking less of myself; it is thinking of myself less." Keller presents us with the gospel irony we need to think rightly about how to be whole, a concept that will be the Christian's stiffest challenge. The temptation with all of our soul problems is to turn inward, not outward. It makes sense, humanly speaking. Self-esteem is the wisdom of the world.

If you are struggling inwardly, then turn outward. Turn to God. Study Him, not yourself. Esteem Him more than anything else, and you'll begin to change internally. If you throw in a pinch of serving others, you'll speed up the process to wholeness (Mark 10:45; Philippians 2:3–4). It may sound foolish to look to God and others first, but it's the wisdom and power of God working in you (1 Corinthians 1:25). When you are captivated by the character and attributes of our transcendent God who has come to dwell in you, your soul will begin to change, and you will begin thinking of yourself less.

Call to Action

1. Describe your pursuit of God. Is it more than just studying Him? Does it also include how you practically apply what you're learning about Him to your life?

2. Are you characterized by thinking more about yourself or more about God? Please explain your answer.

3. Has your understanding of the Imago Dei trained you to respect all humanity—including yourself? Please explain your answer.

4. Have you learned Paul's lesson from Philippians 4:11–13, that no matter his condition, he was content because he could do everything through Christ who strengthened him? Please explain your answer.

5. A new person in Christ acts like Christ. Will you take the fruit of the Spirit in Galatians 5:22–23 and compare yourself to each element? How do you need to change? Write out a specific and practical plan to transform.

2

The Hidden Agenda

Thinking more about yourself is not the path to freedom. The self-esteem agenda demands that we turn our thoughts onto ourselves, spending even more time thinking about ourselves. The Bible has a counterintuitive message: the more thoughts about God we have, the freer we will be. The path to freedom is not by turning inward but upward and outward as we practice loving God and others more than ourselves, a worldview that is counterintuitive, anti-cultural.

The Beauty Gods

"I hate myself because I am so ugly."

—Mable

"Now, Mable, if you really hated yourself, you would be glad you were ugly. In fact, you may even seek ways to become uglier—if you really hated yourself."
—Counselor

This humorous and awkward illustration speaks about our friend, Mable, who fell into the cultural trap of trying to look good, as propagated by the self-esteem gurus who patrol the waters of pop psychology, spreading their soul twisting teaching. The actual truth about Mable is that she is so in love with herself that she hates that she is ugly—according to her perspective. Grading beauty is a cultural phenomenon that changes in accordance with current social norms. The beauty gods manage people like Mable as she craves the proverbial thumbs up, according to the zeitgeist's oscillating winds.

1. Mable looks in the mirror.
1. Mable does not like what she sees.
2. Mable and the culture's view of beauty are at odds.
3. Thus, Mable hates what she sees in the mirror.
4. Conclusion: Mable does not hate herself. She loves herself so much that she hates what she sees in the mirror.

Mable is buying what the culture is selling. She wants to be well-received by her peers, which means she must meet their expectations for beauty. The culture gods motivate Mable to push, press, trim, cut, and paint herself into a mold she hopes they will accept. The people she elevates in her mind to pass judgment on her have power over her. Mable has fallen for self-worship. She is more concerned about peoples' opinions of her than God's thoughts about her. The fear of man has more power over her than the fear of God (Proverbs 29:25). Public opinion and God's opinion are at war in her mind. Her culture teaches the self-actualized person, a teaching that mandates a high view of herself. The self-esteem movement is one of the central planks in her platform. The counterintuitive teaching of the Bible cuts across the grain of the culture's platform.

Through a Biblical Lens

I had heard of you by the hearing of the ear, but now my eye sees you; therefore I despise myself, and repent in dust and ashes.

(Job 42:5–6)

We have all become like one who is unclean, and all our righteous deeds are like a polluted garment. We all fade like a leaf, and our iniquities, like the wind, take us away.

(Isaiah 64:6)

As it is written: None is righteous, no, not one; no one understands; no one seeks for God. All have turned aside; together, they have become worthless; no one does good, not even one.

(Romans 3:10–12)

The saying is trustworthy and deserving of full acceptance, that Christ Jesus came into the world to save sinners, of whom I am the foremost.

(1 Timothy 1:15)

The heart is deceitful above all things, and desperately sick; who can understand it?

(Jeremiah 17:9)

Self-esteem is a call to admire yourself—the person those Scriptures describe. This unbiblical teaching blinds many Christians because they believe it is the solution for their problems, particularly those who struggle with guilt, shame, fear, or insecurity. From a biblical perspective, the term low self-esteem has some inherent problems. For example, if low self-esteem were the problem with an individual like Mable, their solution would be for her to elevate her self-admiration. Do you see anything wrong with this solution compared to the verses you read? Loving herself more would lead her to more painful self-consciousness or delusions of grandeur—thinking she is somebody when, in reality, she is not. If not liking herself was the problem, thinking more about herself would not set her free but only further enslave her. One of the deceptions of self-esteem is to spend more time thinking about ourselves when thoughts of ourselves will consume us.

I Must Increase

Elevating our self-esteem leads to individualism. Individualism leads to an ungodly competitiveness, which pits people against people. One of the ways Mable thinks better about herself is to compare herself to others. She picks them apart to find their flaws. Self-esteem leads to loving God less while looking down on your neighbor with all your heart, soul, mind, and strength. We cannot love God and others more than ourselves when we're trying to elevate ourselves through self-admiration, which can only happen by the ungodly de-admiration of others. Mable's pursuit of high self-esteem diminishes the two greatest commandments (Matthew 22:36–40).

To be a good self-esteemer, we must allow others to control us by their opinion of us. This twisted inversion is why Mable's appearance paralyzes her. She needs positive feedback from others to convince her that she is acceptable. If others put her down, make fun of her, or say she's ugly, it would damage her high self-esteem agenda. She would have to go back to the drawing board, doubling down on changing herself into something that others would find more appealing to entice them to accept her. This process is an exhausting feedback loop.

I Must Decrease

The fear of man lays a snare, but whoever trusts in the LORD *is safe.*

(Proverbs 29:25)

Self-esteem is adjacent to shame, and shame is in the geographical region of the fear of others, also known as insecurity, co-dependency, or peer pressure. It is a person controlled or intimidated by the opinions, perspectives, or views that others have about them. What others think of the self-esteemer has more controlling power over that person than what God thinks of them. Fear of man or insecurity elevates man's opinion above the opinion of God. Insecurity says, "I will feel better if you like me. If you reject me, I will feel bad. I need you to like me." If feeling good about yourself is dependent upon the attitude of others toward you, your friends will control your thoughts and emotions as they let you know what they think about you. If they tell you that you are cool, you feel good. If they tell you that you're uncool or give you the thumbs down, you feel bad.

If you buy into the culture's version of shame—low self-esteem, you're moving headlong into a trap. The answer is not how people view us. The answer is an ever-increasing awareness that we are naked before God, and He must clothe us in the righteousness of Jesus Christ (Genesis 3:7). If our thoughts about ourselves consume us, our problem is not low self-esteem. It's high self-esteem. A low estimation of ourselves implies thinking of ourselves less. Jesus is the most remarkable example of this (Philippians 2:5–11). Self-forgetfulness is the perfect mental attitude for serving others (Mark 10:45).

A Case Study

Mable's mind was an endless feedback loop of self-thought. She wondered what people thought about her. She would tell you what people thought about her. She carefully measured her words so others would accept her. She feared wearing the wrong clothes, hoping never to be out of step with her culture. You would never see her without makeup, always presenting herself perfectly to her anyone. Mable lived in an entangling maze of painful self-awareness. Whenever she left a social gathering, she went into her mind-reading routine, assuming the thoughts of others about her. Her carefully constructed and often wrong interpretations led to more despair. It would mortify Mable to know that people rarely gave her much thought at all. Her friends were far too busy thinking about themselves than thinking about her, the ultimate irony of the self-esteem movement. Christians spend their days esteeming God and others, counting them more significant (Philippians 2:3-4). Our cultural counterparts do not.

Secular Counseling

During her first counseling session, the secular counselor told Mable that she suffered from low self-esteem. He attempted to motivate her to think more highly of herself but was unwittingly leading her into an inescapable trap. Mable was already consumed with herself. The counselor pushed her back into her prison of self-preoccupation. The more Mable gazed into her inner conflict in an attempt to wrap a positive mental attitude around her self-loathing, the more inward and awkward she became. Her unabated social awkwardness only affirmed what she already believed about herself: she was exactly what she thought others thought of her. It's confirmation bias. As the weeks passed, Mable became exasperated, exhausted, and isolated from her world. High self-esteem is an isolating, individualistic, self-centered worldview, not a communal one. Mable withdrew from others. Christ-focused, other-centeredness would have led her back to the community.

Though Mable lived in a real community, she mentally checked out, hiding in plain sight. Three months after her initial counseling session, Mable committed suicide. The report in the local newspaper said she suffered from low self-esteem. Mable suffered from the blinding and penetrating force of high self-esteem. Her thoughts about herself went off the high end of the self-esteem chart. While hiding from others, she became a twisted, self-absorbed, irritable person who found no reason to live. She inevitably turned so inward that there seemed to be no hope from her perspective. Unfortunately for Mable, she was looking in the wrong direction. A person beholding to the high self-esteem mantra runs headlong into the trap of insatiable individualism as they elevate their thoughts to dangerous levels of self-awareness.

Look Up, Not In

Mable needed to look outside herself to rest in the reality of someone far superior to herself. Christ is the answer for inner contentment and outer significance. To be in Christ is to be all you can be, which is your best life now. Jesus came to rescue us from ourselves, not to turn us into ourselves. Looking inward to elevate our estimation of ourselves will lead anyone to dizzying disappointment. Mable attempted to self-talk her way into attaining the unattainable height of all she could be but was left empty. From her perspective, there was no reason to live. She thought she was heading for the light. She was self-deceived, which led to self-enslavement, which led to self-harm. She walked into the darkness of her inner turmoil, never knowing about the Savior who frees captives (Luke 4:18).

If anyone would come after me, let him deny himself and take up his cross and follow me. For whoever would save his life will lose it, but whoever loses his life for my sake will find it.

(Matthew 16:24–25)

Try Self-Worth

- John the Baptist said, "He must increase, but I must decrease" (John 3:30).
- Paul the apostle said, "I am the chief of sinners" (1 Timothy 1:15).

Do you think John or Paul struggled with a lack of self-worth? If you asked them, what would they say? First of all, you would have to explain self-worth to them since that language became part of our vocabulary during the latter decades of the last century. From a Christian historical perspective, self-worth was not a common consideration or a regular part of a Christian's understanding and application of sanctification. Any Christian who argues for a prominent place for self-worth in our understanding and practice of sanctification is making a mountain out of a molehill because the Bible does not speak to this issue in the way they are arguing.

Their primary argumentation comes from the influence of psychology books written in the 20th century. The closest you can find self-worth in the Bible is God making us in His image. Everyone is made in God's image (Genesis 1:27), though it is wrong to put the point of emphasis on the word image rather than God. Being made in the image of God would be of no value if God were not valuable. For example, a painting finds its value from the artist who painted it. If the artist is famous, the painting is valuable. The point of emphasis is primarily on the painter of a famous painting, not the painting. When you walk into a museum to adore a painting,

- You could say, "I saw self portrait, open-mouthed."
- Or you could say, "I saw a Rembrandt."

The first is a painting circa 1630. The second is the painter who painted the portrait. Rembrandt is what makes the painting famous. What makes us so valuable is that God made us in His image. To carve out a psychological doctrine that emphasizes us is wrongheaded. The main point is always about the Creator, not the creation. When the point of emphasis drifts from the artist who made the image to the image itself, we are more psychological than theological. The more sinister possibility is that we will become like Mable, a worshiper of the creature more than the Creator (Romans 1:21–25).

Call to Action

In my counseling experience with insecure people, I have never found a person work their way out of insecure thought patterns without taking John's advice: "He must increase, but I must decrease" (John 3:30). If you are shy, insecure, co-dependent, or struggle with peer pressure, the biblical term for all of those issues is fear of man. If that is you, I appeal to you to learn how to think of yourself less while thinking of God more. If thoughts about God consume you, you are on the path to freedom. The painting feels good about itself when the painter walks into the room. Like the sheep looking at its Shepherd, saying, "The LORD is my shepherd, I shall not want" (Psalm 23:1).

1. Do the opinions of other people control you? Why or why not?
2. If they do, who is the person who has that kind of control over you? Who is it that you're trying to impress or hoping they will like you enough not to reject you?
3. Why do you give them the power to manage you?
4. How does God think about you?
5. What effect does God's opinion of you have on you?
6. Are you characterized as a worshiper of the Painter or the painting? Please explain your answer.

3

On Being Worthless

If you isolate a portion of Scripture from the narrative of the Bible's story, you can misunderstand its meaning, complicating your life and triggering our unregenerate friends. Isolating texts is why some Christians struggle with many of the Bible's declarations. Being worthless is one of those declarations. Imagine lifting Paul's words about us from its context, isolating it from the whole counsel of God. It could be devastating. What did Paul mean? Why is such a harsh perspective on humanity essential to our ultimate good?

A Snowflake Era

Part of the problem with Paul's pronouncement is that we've lost our toughness, along with a dose of myopia. We live in an era where sensitivity is at an all-time high. I'm not suggesting anyone should be harsh or unkind, but there are aspects to our lives that need clarity because some of God's words and descriptors will dig into the foundation of self-actualized souls beholding to such ideologies as the self-esteem movement. When I was a child, it was common to tell someone they were going to hell if they did not trust God. It was not harsh to say it that way, assuming our motives were proper; it was a compassionate appeal. Bad news always precedes good news. Index forward fifty years, and you have a psychologized culture that is highly sensitive and easily offended if you tell them anything that stirs up a negative self-evaluation. Even the Christian resists negative assessments. All our personality tests tell us how uniquely wonderful we are. We cannot help but flatter ourselves while rejecting anything that sounds demeaning.

The culture has drifted so far from the shore of truth that it cannot understand God, and His Word is obscure to them. They pull the scraps of the Bible that they do know through a psychologized filter to soothe the soul with palatable relabeling. The culture's drift is why Paul's words in Romans 3:12 sound like a horrible accusation that threatens how we prefer to think about ourselves. Paul's words in the raw will jar the post-modern psychologized mind. Guess what? It's supposed to jolt us from our hyper-sensory slumber. One purpose of God's Word is to knock us down, which Paul called rebuke or reprove (2 Timothy 3:16). You might want to brace yourself, particularly if you have one of those psychologized minds. Are you ready? Paul said, "All have turned aside; together they have become worthless; no one does good, not even one" (Romans 3:12).

PMA All the Way!

To the secular ear, his words are repulsive, misguided, and threatening, not to mention archaic. To the untrained Christian ear, his words sound about the same. Both demographics are beholding to the self-esteem gospel. Neither group can dare think poorly about themselves. If you are told repeatedly, through a zillion means, that negative evaluations harm your soul, you have no choice but to deny Paul's words or reinterpret what he intended while embracing the culture's version of self-generated, self-actualized goodness. There is no question that Paul's words are disconcerting and even discouraging, which is why isolating them from the rest of God's Word is unwise. We have to contextualize Paul's language between Genesis and Revelation. If we do not, the doctrine of self-esteem will trigger the undiscerning soul.

The culture demands we reject anything contrary to a Positive Mental Attitude (PMA). We cannot call our sports teams the Indians or Redskins because it's detrimental to the psyche, so say, the woke cohort of privileged non-Indian people. In a prior chapter, I talked about how the Christian bases his view of himself on the Imago Dei, the "made in the image of God" concept, rather than the culture's doctrine of self-esteem. The image of God presuppositional worldview keeps our thoughts aligned and in tune with God's Word. The self-esteem worldview leaves the insatiable soul with the culture's solutions to wholeness. Notice in the graphic how the lens through which we see the world creates the commentary for what we believe. If our presuppositional window is God's Word, we will have ultimate clarity, keeping us from drooling and derailing over the secular systems.

Presuppositional Truth

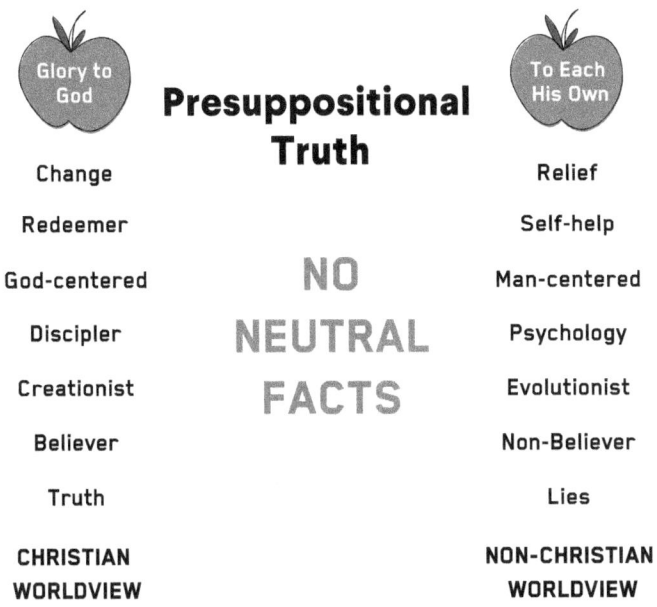

CHRISTIAN WORLDVIEW	Presuppositional Truth	NON-CHRISTIAN WORLDVIEW
Glory to God		To Each His Own
Change		Relief
Redeemer		Self-help
God-centered	NO	Man-centered
Discipler	NEUTRAL	Psychology
Creationist	FACTS	Evolutionist
Believer		Non-Believer
Truth		Lies

Because self-esteem is a secular doctrine born outside of God's Word, all of its solutions are worldly. Our starting point determines our ending point, making understanding presuppositional truth essential. God's Word has a radically different starting point, but it is not Romans 3:12 where we learn about our worthlessness. In Genesis 1:27, we see that God made humanity in the image of the Trinity. The next big thing on the calendar of human events was the marring of God's creation in Genesis 3:6. Adam and Eve chose to walk away from God, which led humanity into a worthless condition (Romans 3:10–12, 5:12; Revelation 20:15). The theological term is total depravity, pointing to complete brokenness spiritually and physically. The goal of Paul's language was not to damage a fragile psyche but to enlighten it while pointing the sad soul to the hope of the gospel. Worthlessness is the condition of every person. Let me illustrate.

Suppose you bought a brand-new vehicle and drove it off the showroom floor. The car is perfect and beautiful in every way. Index forward thirty years. That brand-new automobile sits in the junkyard. It's worn out, broken down, and has "become worthless," to use Paul's language. What was once a fantastic vehicle, built by a master craftsman, is now in the salvage yard. You pass by, look at the car, shake your head, and say, "It has become worthless." If a post-modern car could talk, it would say, "You can't say that about me. I'm not worthless. I'm somebody. Do you see the snowflakes on my windshield? You are damaging my car esteem." You respond, "Think what you want about yourself, but you have become worthless. You may have been something once upon a time, but you are not that any longer, and if you want to rise from this junkyard, it will not happen by the mirage of self-generated value and self-reliant means. You need outside intervention."

Bad Precedes Good

The Master Craftsman chose to make us in His image (Psalm 139:14), but humanity took a devilish turn in the garden of Eden (Genesis 3:6). Humanity landed in the junk heap of life (Ezekiel 16:6). Our condition is so bad that any good thing we do is filthy and marred (Isaiah 64:6). We became worthless. The secular person puts his psychological fingers in his ears while saying unkind things to anyone who would make such a horrible declaration. Our condition prior to regeneration is also repulsive to some Christians. They refuse to see themselves the way God does, post-fall, pre-redemption. They misunderstand and misapply God's Word in the most practical ways. To think we are something is forbidding Christ from our lives because He came for the sick, broken, contrite, humble, and self-aware; He came for the worthless. There is no doubt it would be the most horrible of tragedies if any of us were stuck in Romans 3:12.

To be worthless and left in that state is a desperate and depressing condition, which explains why the culture is so extreme, competing and tromping all over each other in the pursuit of creating something (anything) that gives them a fleeting feeling of self-importance. If you follow sports, you see this all the time as the prima-donna athlete does all kinds of stunts after a great play to create a buzz that will pump up his inflatable ego through the next twenty-four-hour news cycle. It's a shallow and sad fifteen seconds of fame. The Christian does not have to compete in such nonsensical exercises to fill a fictitious love cup because he knows what Paul said in Romans 3:12 is the condition and position that sets him up for God's supernatural intervention. Christ is looking for the worthless beggar. God is interested in totally depraved people who name it and claim it, not those who shame it and defame it.

Rest of the Story

That kind of humble seeker is ready for grace. He knows God made him in His image (Genesis 1:27), that he became worthless (Romans 3:10), and God must restore him to the beauty that only His grace can provide. The bad news does not damage his psyche; it positions him for the best news a sad soul will ever hear. The Christian is exempt from a sin-centered, worm-centered, worthless theology, which is what would happen if Romans 3:12 was his irreconcilable, unending condition. A worthless vehicle with no means of escaping the junkyard is in a horrible place. The believer knows the rest of the story. He pleads for the second birth because his first one landed him in the junkyard of life (Romans 5:12).

The God rejector stays a totally depraved, worthless sinner with no hope of extricating himself from his iniquity. He may listen to the words of Jesus: "You must be born again" (John 3:7), but he won't budge. Regeneration is something the secularist will never do. God will leave him to his own devices, which is why the self-esteem doctrine is readily available and appreciated for those without hope. A second birth is the perfect antidote to rescue anyone from the junkyard. God will restore you to what you were supposed to be—a regenerated Imago Dei. Being born again does more than restore us to what we should be; it guarantees no more reversals. For the Christian, the whole story is a three-part narrative.

1. **CREATION:** God made us in His image.
2. **FALL:** We became worthless because of sin.
3. **REDEMPTION:** God restores us by His power.

Regeneration is an unusual turn of events—all brought to you by the power and grace of God, not by a twisted self-esteem doctrine that sends you into a hopeless maze of artificial feel-good so you can psyche yourself up to be something you can never be outside of divine mercy and intervention. God contextualizes our hope in His power rather than secular contrivances. Salvation gives hope and practical help to the desperate soul. If you are born again, you're on the path to complete restoration. You're not there yet, but you're on the track, which is why Paul had so much optimism for the troubled Corinthians.

> [God] who will sustain you to the end, guiltless in the day of our Lord Jesus Christ. God is faithful, by whom you were called into the fellowship of his Son, Jesus Christ our Lord.
>
> (1 Corinthians 1:8–9)

Hope for the Helpless

Think about what Paul said to this corrupt and broken group of people. Sin owned them, but Paul knew the end of the story, so he could say they would be guiltless on the day of the Lord. You could say it this way, "No matter what you're going through or what you're struggling with now, be assured that you will be okay because what God begins, He finishes" (Philippians 1:6). Paul was talking to the Christians in Corinth. He knew God created them in His image, but they had become worthless. Paul also knew they were born again. His robust theology did not deny the extreme realities of the human condition, which is why he was so full of faith in how things would end for the Corinthians: they would be guiltless in eternity.

The self-esteem doctrine does not give that kind of hope. At best, it insists the proponent must pump up himself daily with an "I am somebody, I am somebody, I am somebody" mantra that propels the Bible rejector out the door with a "go, fight, win" attitude. He is only as great as his latest victory. Christians are different. We do not base our view of ourselves on our latest and greatest achievements. It's also not based on other people respecting or rejecting us. We do not live or die by the latest polling data. We build our hope on nothing less than Jesus Christ and His righteousness. This worldview is not myopic like the self-esteemer, but it is a faith in God that sustains us throughout this life while preparing us for unending future satisfaction.

Call to Action

1. Why does Paul's declaration about being worthless come across as so harsh? How does it sound to you and why?
2. Some of the best news you'll ever hear is that you're in the worthless junkyard of life and cannot do anything to rescue yourself. Why is that?
3. Which is more important to you: better self-esteem or the Bible's three-part restoration process of being made in God's image, becoming worthless, and the Lord restoring you? Please explain your answer.
4. How important is it for you to have the praise and appreciation of others? How much do those things manage you? Describe the person who finds satisfaction in God's favorable opinion of him or her because of regeneration.

4

From Bad to Good

One of the most counterintuitive messages for anyone to accept is their inherent badness. Many people already think poorly about themselves so they will not accept more condemnation, never realizing how overcoming what's wrong with them is affirming those negative thoughts. If you think poorly of yourself, you're on the right path to wholeness. The Bible's declaration is we are worthless. We are not good people. The culture says you are somebody. They believe that people are inherently good. The Bible says we're not that special, though I'm not speaking of self-worth that flows from the Imago Dei but a futile worldly belief system that says we are good people and do not need Christ's alien righteousness. Let me illustrate.

Love Me Like I Do

Biff is depressed and discouraged. He keeps saying, "I'm not good enough; I wish I were a better person. I want to be a good person." Over and over again, like a yoga mantra: "I am not good enough; I wish I were a good person. I am so unworthy. I have done so many horrible things. How could Christ love me?" Do you hear what he is saying? Do you see the problem with his theology and how he practicalizes it? What if we put his self-flagellating statements through a theological filter?

I am a terrible person. I am so bad that God cannot possibly love me. If I were not so bad, maybe God would love me. I need to be a better person. I need to make myself more presentable than I am so God will like me.

Biff is explaining—unwittingly—his functional theology. Ironically, he has an intellectual theology that says,

For by grace you have been saved through faith. And this is not your own doing; it is the gift of God, not a result of works, so that no one may boast.
(Ephesians 2:8–9)

The Ephesian text is what Biff knows (informational), but it is not what Biff practically trusts, where it matters the most. What he understands is not transformational. It is challenging sometimes for people to distinguish between what they know (Bible truth) and what they are authentically practicing—their practical theology.

I'm Okay; You're Okay

I was talking with my friend [Mable], a drug addict. She tried her best to convince me that she was a good person. She said the quiet part aloud, "I am a good person." Mable hoped that when we ended our conversation, I would walk away thinking she was a good person. People like Mable are needy. They need others to agree with their self-imposed high self-estimation of themselves. Their high self-esteem demands our obedience. To maintain her delusion, she needs me to agree with her. It could go like this:

Please love me the way I love me so I can keep this love that I have for myself. If you love me, I will feel good about myself. If you don't love me, I will feel bad about myself. I need you to love me. Will you love me? If you

don't, you will force me to find someone else to love me because I need people to love me in order for me to feel good about myself.

I chose not to tell Mable what I was thinking at that moment. It was not appropriate or helpful for me to teach her sound theology, especially the doctrines of humanity, sin, and salvation. She was not ready to receive the testimony of Scripture:

The saying is trustworthy and deserving of full acceptance that Christ Jesus came into the world to save sinners, of whom I am the foremost.

(1 Timothy 1:15)

Or,

None is righteous, no, not one; no one understands; no one seeks for God. All have turned aside; together, they have become worthless; no one does good, not even one.

(Romans 3:10–12)

Mable does not want to wrestle with the realities of her wretchedness. In her mind, she wants to think of herself as better than what the testimony of the Scriptures says she is and what Christians throughout church history have believed and taught. If only she could convince me of her goodness, things would be okay; she would feel better about herself. If I accepted her perceived goodness, it would doubly affirm her delusional "I'm okay, you're okay" fixation. Her worldview is the damnableness of our culture's self-esteem teaching.

The Bad and the Ugly

The culture teaches nobody can be wrong, everybody should feel good about themselves, and nobody should lose. "Hey, loser, you get a trophy too." They believe negative waves damage our self-esteem. The Bible appeals to us to think of ourselves less, which is the only way to be truly free (Matthew 20:20–28). Both Biff and Mable do not want to think biblically. They do not want to be unworthy. Biff is a Christian, and Mable is not, but they both struggle similarly. They are self-righteous, which is a greater than/better than attitude. For them to change, it will be vital for them to accept that they are wretchedly unworthy of God's favor. There is no other way for them to receive His unearned, unmerited grace.

> And when Jesus heard it, he said to them, "Those who are well have no need of a physician, but those who are sick. I came not to call the righteous, but sinners."
>
> (Mark 2:17)

Self-esteem entangles their thinking. They are not as good as they try to deceive themselves and others into believing. Have you ever expected a good grade only to get a bad one? In a sense, that is what Biff and Mable fear. They so badly want an excellent grade, but they keep failing, and their unwillingness to embrace the reality of their inability distresses them. They distance themselves from the testimony of God's Word while developing a practical theology that holds them to a higher standing than what the Bible declares. They persist in convincing themselves of their "higher grade worthiness," though the reality of their lives is not cooperating with what they try to gaslight themselves and others into believing.

Embracing Unworthiness

Their strategy is a trap that somebody will have to walk them through if they hope to be free from themselves and from needing others. It won't be easy to help them. When Biff sees who he is, discouragement settles into his mental stronghold. Mable is similar. When she surveys the sordid landscape of her life, she becomes discouraged. Her reactive response as she wallows in the grips of depression is drugs. Her pick-me-up effort to elevate herself eventually drives her soul into despair. Because Biff is a Christian, he won't turn to such ungodly escapes as drugs. He puts himself through the cycles of self-pity and despair. In the end, both of them have an addiction. One is addicted to illegal drugs, and the other is addicted to a delusional high view of himself.

Neither of them can lift themselves by their bootstraps, so they turn to their drugs of choice. Biff and Mable must come to terms with their unworthiness before God. They are putrid through and through. They are the worst of the worst, the lowest of the low. When you hear such things, does your mind begin to think about the victory you have in Christ or how horrible and damaging that kind of thinking is? The gospel-centered person has ears to hear and quickly indexes forward to his victory in Christ. He does not see a commentary about unworthiness as depressing but as a necessary step in getting to Christ. The self-righteous person will disdain being unworthy while touting his strengths and accolades. He may whip out his latest personality test to exalt his positive uniqueness.

> We have all become like one who is unclean, and all
> our righteous deeds are like a polluted garment. We
> all fade like a leaf, and our iniquities, like the wind,
> take us away.
>
> (Isaiah 64:6)

For Biff and Mable, the biblical path upward is not to climb out of their total depravity by their own power. They must begin the process of a total makeover by shouting, "Amen, I am a terrible person and cannot fix myself."

God the Justifier

Without question, we were pitifully guilty before the Lord. We were standing in God's courtroom, condemned, awaiting sentencing. Undoubtedly, we were responsible for the greatest crime ever committed. We sinned against God. The evidence was irrefutable. We stopped our mouths, and there was not a thing we could do to extricate ourselves from the accusation of evil that was against us. Though we wanted to think better about ourselves to feel better about ourselves, there was no argument we could proffer. God, the Prosecuting Attorney, made the evidence plain, convincing, and beyond any shadow of a doubt. We were guilty before our Maker, and we were at His mercy. Self-salvation was not an option.

> But now the righteousness of God has been manifested apart from the law, although the Law and the Prophets bear witness to it—the righteousness of God through faith in Jesus Christ for all who believe. For there is no distinction: for all have sinned and fall short of the glory of God, and are justified by his grace as a gift, through the redemption that is in Christ Jesus.
>
> (Romans 3:21–24)

In the depths of our despair and unworthiness, we learned about the most incredible news ever told. The gospel story came into view. We were sightings of Calvary. There is only one answer for unworthy people: embrace the worthiness of another. The sick and helpless cry out to the physician. Biff is a believer who needs to reacquaint himself with the old gospel story. He needs to understand what the doctrine of justification means practically. God, the Judge, slammed the gavel down and said, "Not guilty!" That was it. Jesus finished it. Biff was legally declared not guilty by the Judge of the universe. He was free when Christ took his unrighteousness and gave him His righteousness, what we call an alien righteousness.

Flipping Justification

There was nothing else for Biff to do, and there never will be anything else for him to do. God Almighty declared him innocent, not because he conjured up some merit that won God over to his side. To the contrary. Christ won the Father over through His sacrificial death on Biff's behalf. The works of Christ persuaded the Father to accept Biff as His dear son. Mable can do that too, but first, she needs her initial acquaintance with the gospel in a salvific way (John 3:7). She needs to hear and embrace the good news about the Savior's atoning death. She needs to believe His death was for her, and she can only be the good person she presently deceives herself to be through Christ alone. Biff and Mable have flipped justification and sanctification in their thinking and practice.

Justification always precedes sanctification and is not dependent on sanctification. According to Biff's and Mable's practical theology, they believe that sanctification precedes justification. Their sanctification—good works and behaviors—makes them right with God and before others. They think that if they can work enough or do the right things, they will be acceptable (or justified). They feel better about themselves through their effort, requiring a daily ritual of proving acceptability. Biff will argue with you because he is a Christian and knows Ephesians 2:8-9. You will have to carefully walk him through how he functionally practices his theology, which is contrary to the Bible and what he knows intellectually. He embraces a form of legalism: a person who feels good about himself because of what he does. The goal would be to help him see three things.

1. His ongoing self-pity about his badness is wrongheaded.
2. He must accept His badness to see his genuine need for the One who is perfectly good.
3. Once he repents from his self-imposed righteousness—high self-esteem, he will be able to receive God's unearned mercy.

Reflect on this graphic. Notice how justification stands alone and is not dependent upon sanctification. But sanctification always connects to and flows from justification.

Justification & Sanctification Compared

GIVEN FREELY BY GOD'S GRACE	GIVEN FREELY BY GOD'S GRACE
GIVEN BY FAITH	GIVEN BY FAITH
FOUND ONLY IN THE SAVED	FOUND ONLY IN THE SAVED
IS THE WORK OF CHRIST	IS THE WORK OF CHRIST
DISTINCT FROM SANCTIFICATION	LINKED TO JUSTIFICATION
AN ACT	A WORK
LEGAL DECLARATION	LIVING OUT IN RIGHTEOUSNESS
IS CHRIST FOR US	IS CHRIST IN US
PASSIVE ACTION	ACTIVE ACTION
HAPPENS AT POINT IN TIME	A PROGRESSIVE WORK
OUR STANDING (I AM SAVED)	MORAL LIFE: DEVELOPING CHARACTER
STANDING IS PERFECT	STANDING IS BEING PERFECTED
POSITIONAL	PRACTICAL
CANNOT BE SEEN	CAN BE SEEN

Shiny Diamonds

The saying is trustworthy and deserving of full acceptance, that Christ Jesus came into the world to save sinners, of whom I am the foremost. But I received mercy for this reason, that in me, as the foremost, Jesus Christ might display his perfect patience as an example to those who were to believe in him for eternal life.

(1 Timothy 1:15–16)

Some people believe that if you talk about your badness all of the time, you are sin-centered and there is no grace in your life. I agree: you are sin-centered, and strictly sin-centered thinking mocks Calvary. However, Paul had no qualms about announcing to the world at the end of his life that he was the chief of sinners, though he did not fixate on his badness. Yes, he was the worst of the worst and bad to the bone, but he also tells us that God showed mercy to him. Jerry Bridges said, and I paraphrase, "A diamond is most magnificent when placed against a black, velvet backdrop." So true. The more you are aware of your badness and hopeless ability to repair your wretchedness, the more you will be strengthened by the grace of God. If you are unwilling to accept the testimony of Scripture regarding your badness, you will limit and truncate the powerful grace that God offers to humble, broken, and unworthy people.

Call to Action

1. Do you understand and embrace your badness? Please explain.
2. Does your awareness tempt you to present yourself as good, or does it propel you to accept the righteousness of Christ alone? Please explain.
3. When you do bad things, are you tempted to balance the scales by doing good things—a self-reliant attempt to renew a better standing with God? Please explain.
4. When you do bad things, do you run to the only good person who can make it right? If you don't do this, why not?
5. Did you know your good works do not make you any more saved, and your evil works do not make you any less saved? Will you share your response with a friend?

5

Getting over Ourselves

One of the most challenging things a person will ever do is tell others the secrets of who they really are. I'm not suggesting we blab all our stuff to everyone, or even our deepest, darkest secrets that only God knows, but there is wisdom in inviting at least one trusted friend into our more vulnerable thought lives, a person who can handle our unsavory truth. Ironically, many Christians will not do this even though we're all messed up. Nobody is perfect, as we like to say. To bums on the street not talking about what is apparent to both of them is odd.

Set the Imperfect Free

Imperfect people are afraid to share their imperfections with other imperfect people. Does that strike you as odd? It's like a skunk being afraid to tell another skunk that he stinks. We all stink. Rather than embracing the biblical record—we smell bad; we seek to perfume ourselves to make ourselves appear better than we know ourselves to be. We're like a bunch of skunks seeking to fake out each other. It's somewhat weird. Wouldn't being set free from people-pleasing, image-guarding, and reputation management be a better option? I recognize that some people do not have that trusted, intimate friend while others fear the risks of relationships. We live in a fallen world; sometimes, it can take longer than we had hoped to reach the ideals of God's Word. How free are you?

- Are you open to sharing your secrets appropriately? Or are you tempted to cover up and hide your truest self?
- If you are, in what ways do you hide?
- How do you make yourself appear better than you know yourself to be?
- What are your tricks of the repetitional management trade?
- Do you see how the charade is vain, leaves you empty, and feeds low levels of discontentedness?
- If this is you, what would it take to release you from this bondage? What steps will you take to find that trusted friend?

Do You Smell?

For all have sinned and fall short of the glory of God.
(Romans 3:23)

I think if we were honest with ourselves, we would agree with the Bible's perspective about ourselves and accept its truth claims: we are sinners through and through—totally depraved. If we were humble and courageous, we would openly discuss how we struggle with sin with our intimate friends. Not only have we sinned, but it gets worse: others have sinned against us. Sin happens in two ways: we sin; people sin against us. We are active sinners and passive, unwelcome recipients of other people's sins. On one level, it does not matter how we got this way. Whether it was our doing, Adam's doing, or the fault of others, there is something profoundly wrong with us.

And when Jesus heard it, he said to them, "Those who are well have no need of a physician, but those who are sick. I came not to call the righteous, but sinners."

(Mark 2:17)

The thing we have to guard against is how we respond to our internal dysfunction. It would be better to accept the truth about our unique smells, recognizing that we all stink to high heaven. The gospel already tells us we are badly broken and need repair. Isn't that the point and purpose of the gospel? Didn't He come to repair broken people? Christ is our divine repairman. Sometimes, some people spend too much time figuring out how they got to their current dysfunction. Deliberating to discern our active role or our passive receiving in our dysfunction is not the best use of our time. The primary concern is what we are doing to repair ourselves. What is your repair plan? A person who can accept that he has a problem can quickly transition to gospel solutions for his mess-up-ness rather than wasting his days blaming others for how he got to where he is. The free individual is not concerned about who he is, what he did, or who did what to him.

Who Is Fixing You?

The free person has moved forward because he accepts the truth claims of the Bible—he is a sinner. Say it aloud: "I am a messed-up person." Did you say it? Good. Now, let's move on. The real struggle is how we fix ourselves. Who is repairing us, and how is it happening? One of the biggest temptations for messed-up people is to fall prey to the do-it-yourself self-repair worldview. Let me introduce you to seven people born into sin like us. They are active sinners and the unwanted recipients of sin from others. From a sin perspective, they are the same but seek different ways of self-repair.

- Mable's fix-it approach was to enhance her natural beauty. She became a flirt who enjoyed capturing the gaze of guys. It made her feel robust, durable, and unbroken inside. Sadly, when she pillows her head at night, the gnawing reality of the emptiness of her soul causes her to toss and turn. Her self-repair methodology is only as deep as her make-up.
- Biff pushed through three degree programs. You only have to spend five minutes with Biff to learn about his education. Academics is his identity. His feel-good-about-himself syndrome is three diplomas thin.
- Bert went the bodybuilding route. He is one strong-looking, macho man. Just don't let him know that you know his hulkiness is a weak disguise. He has a significant anger problem, as you might imagine, which, combined with his physique, keeps the undiscerning cowering or impressed.
- Marge became an athlete because she could. It was her strength. It became her surefire way to gain attention, significance, acceptance, and approval. After she blew out her ACL, her world collapsed. The injury took away her self-repair kit. She lost hope. She became a drug addict. Nothing mattered to her anymore, and it still doesn't.
- Madge went into the ministry. In her mind, it compensated for the hideousness of what she did as a teen. According to her accounting, having sex is one of the worst sins a person could commit; therefore, going into the ministry is one of the best things she could do. Ministry made things right in her self-atoning mind. She will tell you that her salvation is by grace, not by works, but her practical theology reveals a legalistic heart condition.
- Myrtle is on her third husband. The dating and early marriage process work great for her. She loves being pursued, captured, and loved by a man. After she got

her love cup filled to overflowing, she realized she married a selfish person—her clone, who is more about receiving than giving. Myrtle is one angry and frustrated lady in search of number four.

- Bart is thirty-five years old now and still living at home. He knows it's twisted, but it's safe. Why try anything if there is a risk of failure? Each time he fails, he has to endure the painful reminders of inadequacy, the complications of the fear of man, and a more than subtle reality that he can't fix himself. Regardless, he chooses not to try rather than to try and fail.

Whose Works?

All seven of these people realized something was wrong with them; they stink to high heaven like the rest of us. All seven tried man-centered, man-glorifying ways to overcome their souls' shame/guilt dynamic. All seven put on a front of having it together, which worked to varying degrees, depending on their ability to pull off their charades. All seven of them are miserable. All seven of them have not come to embrace the liberating truth claims of the gospel. Every person receives two options for their transformation. Option one takes you down the road of self-effort, self-help, self-reliance, and self-centeredness, as these seven people have done. Option two takes you down the path of dying to yourself while relying on someone more special and effective. There is no question it will take much work to fix personal brokenness. The real question is, whose works will we rely on for our transformation?

The most evident and natural temptation is to rely on ourselves—like our case study friends. The self-reliant approach is native to all of us. Trusting others is difficult for insecure people, who prefer a self-sufficient "I can do it myself" mantra. Didn't you learn long ago that you can't trust anyone? Don't you know that nobody else will come through for you? Besides, you have gifts, qualities, assets, and strengths. It makes sense to leverage them to your advantage. Others will let you down, but you will never let yourself down. People will not make you feel better about yourself, but self-reliant idolatries can. But did you know an unguarded strength could be your most significant liability? Could it be that your strengths have further incarcerated you? Have you considered that you could be a slave to your God-given abilities to pull yourself up by your bootstraps? These side-effects of self-sufficiency are what can happen with our strengths. Personal gifting can be a tool to enslave ourselves into more profound self-reliance. Anybody who seeks to enhance their reputation because they are overly concerned with what others think about them will be tempted to strengthen themselves through personal abilities. Their mantra is, "I can do all things through me who strengthens me" (Philippians 4:13).

Living in God's Pleasure

Our strengths and abilities may impress others and garner the long-craved approval we desire, but it does not garner the acceptance of God. The Father is not impressed with our works, even if our good deeds are righteous (Isaiah 64:6). God is pleased with the works of His Son (Mark 1:11). It is Jesus who pleases Him. The Lord will never find pleasure in our finely-honed skillset or well-established reputations. He is pleased with His Son's works and reputation. It is His Son's name that He wants to put on display, not ours. If your self-produced reputation gives you the desired approval, do you think you've gained something? Can you see how living for reputation and image enhancement is a vain life? Our seven friends all struggle similarly. They sense stinging guilt deep inside of them. Part of that guilt is what they were born with because of Adam. It's their Adamic problem. Part of their sense of shame came from fellow sinners. People have hurt them. Part of their struggle is their fault.

Rather than trusting and resting in Christ to free them from their internal turmoil, they carved a self-generated path to make themselves feel better about themselves. The end for each of them has left them hollow, empty, and unsatisfied. There is no amount of work we could ever do to satisfy the guilt that is held against us by God. Our guilt is an infinite guilt that demands an infinite payment. Finite people do not have what it takes to pay an infinite price for an infinite transgression. The only way we could pay for our sin against God is to pay it eternally. That is why we have hell. It is for people who do not want to do it God's way but prefer to pay their infinite debt themselves. Mercifully, God gave us another choice, another infinite option for what we have done. God gave Himself—an infinite gift—as a sacrifice for our infinite crime. This kindness from God is the gospel. All He asks us to do is accept His gift. He wants us to cease from our works and enter into His rest.

Live Who You Are

Perhaps you have accepted His gift. Maybe you have been born again. Perhaps the good Lord has paid your sin debt, but there can still be a problem. What I did not tell you about our seven friends is that they all profess Christ. The mercy of God has regenerated them, which raises some big questions.

- Why are they not living in the freedom that the gospel offers?
- Why are they not enjoying their entire inheritance?
- Why are they still seeking to promote their glory and not Christ's?
- Why is the gospel not impacting their sanctification?
- What do they fear?

The gospel has been powerful enough to save them but not to progressively sanctify them. In essence, they are unbelieving believers. They are functional atheists. They are people who the gospel has saved, but the gospel is not practically ruling their hearts. They are still bound to image, reputation, and people-pleasing. These individuals still want to protect, guard, and hide their true selves. They live to impress people as though their stinkiness is something to be proud of among friends. Though they trust Christ, they still want to hold onto pockets of glory.

If this describes you to any degree and you struggle with being honest about who you are and how you need help, here is a prayer for you. Ask the Father to release you from your fear. Let the gospel do more than save you. Let it sanctify you. The best thing you can do is find a trusted friend and reveal your actual heart to them—appropriately. Let them know you are a pretender, and you need help. Let them know what they already know about you: you smell bad. Who knows; your humble and honest transparency may be the key to releasing them from a similar bondage.

Prayer for Stinkers

Dear Father,

I have tried many things to make me feel better about myself. Some of these notions were objectively wrong. Some of them give the perception of righteous deeds. My efforts, good and evil, have closed my eyes to the truths of the gospel.

I have not fully rested in the gospel. I know the truth, and I know that I'm a pretender. Please help me be honest with you and with others. I don't want to do this anymore. I don't want to do evil or good works. I want to rest in your divine pleasure because I trust your Son's works alone.

But I cannot do this alone. I need divine

intervention. Will you give me the faith to live like a set-free Christian? Will you give me the faith to share my struggles? I love you. I love the gospel. Make it real to me and release me from the bondage of self-reliance that my fears perpetuate. Will you bring a friend to help me? I'm a debtor to your mercy.

For you will not delight in sacrifice, or I would give it; you will not be pleased with a burnt offering. The sacrifices of God are a broken spirit; a broken and contrite heart, O God, you will not despise.

(Psalm 51:16–17)

Call to Action

1. Will you have a long-form discussion with a friend about the content in this chapter?
2. If you do not have that friend, will you talk to your pastor, share these things with him, and ask for his assistance finding you a friend?
3. If you do not have a pastor or other spiritual leader you're comfortable talking to, will you speak to God, asking Him to remove any excuses that hinder you from finding this friend so you can have that long-form discussion? Act as though a mature walk with God depends on it because it does.
4. Perhaps returning to my questions at the beginning of this chapter and answering them with a friend will assist you in this journey of faith.
    *   How free are you?
    *   Are you open to sharing your secrets appropriately? Or are you tempted to cover up and hide your truest self?
    *   If you are, in what ways do you hide?
    *   How do you make yourself appear better than you know yourself to be?

- What are your tricks of the repetitional management trade?
- Do you see how the charade is vain, leaves you empty, and feeds low levels of discontentedness?
- If this is you, what would it take to release you from this bondage?
- What steps will you take to find that trusted friend?

5. For a deeper conversation, reflect and answer the questions about our seven reluctant and self-reliant friends:
   - Why are they not living in the freedom that the gospel offers?
   - Why are they not enjoying their entire inheritance?
   - Why are they still seeking to promote their glory and not Christ's?
   - Why is the gospel not impacting their sanctification?
   - What do they fear?

6

Helping the Stuck

Trying to be perfect in an imperfect world to garner the favorable opinion of others is a delusion that will strain any relationship, not to mention how it will bind the soul to a lifetime pursuit of the unfillable love cup. The temptation to be stuck on oneself is native to all of us because of the Adamic shame that creates an internal awkwardness, motivating the hungry searcher to create a personification of themselves to convince others that they are something special when none of us are—outside the grace of God. Let me illustrate how this works with my friend Mable.

Self-righteous Insecurity

Mable is insecure. She has a hard time admitting she is wrong. Mable has a high view of herself, a form of self-righteousness. How she appears before others and brings self-centered commentaries about how others think about her is part of her daily routine. Many of her friends love her; they see Mable as an example they want to emulate. Her family has a different perspective. They can never honestly say what they think about her because Mable has never been humble enough to receive their observations. Insecure people are like this. Whenever her family brings their perspectives about Mable to Mable, she responds with anger or other emotive reactions while letting them know how they failed her. Rather than trying to understand,

Mable's insecurity forces her to turn the tables with unfounded accusations. Mable's family has taken the position of overlooking so much because it is not worth the conflict.

> The way of a fool is right in his own eyes, but a wise man listens to advice.
>
> (Proverbs 12:15)

Mable's self-righteousness has had an even more detrimental effect on her husband, Biff. He has had his sin problems, and Mable has not been shy about reminding him of where he has failed and how he has hurt her. She expresses her disappointment to Biff through her nagging, criticism, and consistent demeaning attitude. Recently, Mable told him if he continued sinning, she would leave him. Biff has been trying to walk out his repentance in humility, and it appears he is doing well with the process. Recently, he said during a counseling session:

> I don't want to sin anymore. I'm working hard not to. I have spent more time in prayer than at any other time in my life. I have been reading the Bible more than ever. I've set up accountability partners to help guard my heart against falling back into sin. Even so, I know there will be times when I will fall. I don't want to do this, and I'm not making excuses, but I'm unsure I can live a life of perfection, which Mable is asking me to do. I know it sounds wrong, but there has been this temptation to lie to Mable when she asks me if I sinned. Do you know what I mean? So, when she asks, "How's it going, Biff?" What am I to say?

Esteeming Yourself

There are many layers and concerns related to Mable's case study. I will only interact with one of the problems presented—her self-righteousness. Self-righteousness is part of the brokenness that comes with being born in Adam. Along with unbelief, shame, guilt, fear, craving for comfort, a desire to be in control, there is also a compulsion to over-estimate ourselves—all parts of who we are as sinful humans. These things are objectively Mable's sin list. All of these things have traces of self-righteous, something that our culture perpetuates through their self-esteem gospel. Those who do not want to submit to the Lord seek other means to feel good about themselves, which typically has something to do with being superior to others. Self-righteousness elevates yourself above others, even if the other person is yourself. Let me explain.

- Self-righteous people look down on others.
- Self-righteous people look down on themselves—the things they do not like about themselves.

We all have enough self-awareness to know that we are not perfect. Something within us motivates us to be better than the people we know ourselves to be. Therefore, we mask our flaws while we promote our more-preferred qualities. This problem implodes inside of us as we sabotage our inner selves by elevating ourselves above others. This attitude is what the Pharisees did in the New Testament. Becoming a Christian does not insulate us from this sin.

> Beware of practicing your righteousness before other people in order to be seen by them.
>
> (Matthew 6:1)

Though we may have accepted the righteousness of Christ as our own, the temptation is to smuggle our righteousness into our lives to build a reputation that can feed our desire for self-glory. The humble Christian is intuitively familiar with this problem. Only a self-righteous person would be offended if someone told them that they were self-righteous. Their high opinion of themselves would motivate them to reject any negative assessment, even if the evaluation were accurate. Confronting the elevated soul is one of the things that makes caring for the self-righteous person so challenging. Their high view of themselves compels them to resist the analysis. Even with the best intentions, they would receive your care as inaccurate, harsh, or unkind, a worldview that makes Paul's self-analysis counterintuitive. He was clear-headed regarding his honest, sober, and biblical self-assessment.

The Chiefest

The saying is trustworthy and deserving of full acceptance, that Christ Jesus came into the world to save sinners, of whom I am the foremost. But I received mercy for this reason, that in me, as the foremost, Jesus Christ might display his perfect patience as an example to those who were to believe in him for eternal life.

(1 Timothy 1:15-16)

He understood and humbly lived in the antithetical juxtaposition of his total depravity and Christ's impeccable righteousness. He was free to drop his denials and self-defenses while admitting the more accurate dimensions of his sin.

The gospel of justifying faith means that while Christians are, in themselves, still sinful and sinning, yet in Christ, in God's sight, they are accepted and righteous. So, we can say that we are more wicked than we ever dared believe, but more loved and accepted in Christ than we ever dared hope—at the very same time. This creates a radical new dynamic for personal growth. It means that the more you see your own flaws and sins, the more precious, electrifying, and amazing God's grace appears to you. But on the other hand, the more aware you are of God's grace and acceptance in Christ, the more able you are to drop your denials and self-defenses and admit the true dimensions and character of your sin.

—Tim Keller

Self-righteous people have not experienced this practical liberation to think about or present themselves as Paul considered himself and lived before others. They continue to guard, protect, and justify on one side while being defensively and fearfully critical, negative, and arrogant on the other side. If you bring any critique to them, you will experience some form of anger that will put you down while elevating themselves over you.

Fear of Man

The fear of man lays a snare, but whoever trusts in the LORD is safe.

(Proverbs 29:25)

The companion sin that hangs out with the self-righteous soul is the fear of others—culturally called co-dependency, insecurity, or people-pleasing. Mable is enslaved and bound by the opinions of others. If you approve of her, she will be your friend. If Mable perceives your disapproval—whether founded or not, she will be your enemy. She hopes you will think about her in the way she thinks about herself, which is a high view of herself. She does not understand and cannot enjoy how the only opinion in the room that should matter is the Lord's opinion of her, and sadly, God's opinion does not control her. The Lord's thoughts of her, as experienced through the application of Christ's righteousness, should be her controlling identity.

She is still under the influence of others. Will you accept me? Please don't reject me. What do you think of me? Her thoughts are all-controlling when she thinks about friends and family, creating an enslaved mindset. Mable hopes others will have a similar view of herself that she has of herself. The primary way she can influence those opinions is through self-promotion, which is the essence of self-righteousness. A person trapped by the fear of others has many symptoms that they employ to cope with their enslavement. Here are a few of Mable's awful habits.

- Oversleeping
- Overeating
- Too much talking
- Easy embarrassment
- Can't be transparent with others
- Is frustrated and discontent
- Avoidance of others
- Self-conscious
- Can't handle rejection well
- Is inflexible
- She has to be in control.
- Afraid of failure
- Exaggeration
- She is reactionary and defensive.
- Competitive with others
- Name dropping
- Must have the last word
- Struggle with oversensitivity
- Confronting people corporately but not personally

Self-assessment

The quickest and most straightforward way to assess a self-righteous person bound to the fear of others is to listen to them. How do they talk to others? How do they respond to others? How do they talk about others? Here are a few questions that have helped me assess my lingering Adamic self-righteousness.

- Am I quick to acknowledge my sins to the right people?
- Am I initially reluctant about acknowledging the sins of others?
- Can I receive a critique?
- Do I actively pursue others for correction?

Here are a few more diagnostic questions that I have benefited from, and I hope they will help you to discern any self-righteousness that may be present in you. All of them are closed-ended, so you want to explain your answers.

- Have you ever been tempted to critique or judge another person, group, or church sinfully?
- How do you usually respond to those who do not do things according to your preferences?
- Do you focus on what you do correctly and what others may do wrong?
- How do you think critically about others living out secondary preferences differently?
- Do you secretly feel smug because God has delivered you from some of the sins you see in others?
- Do you become impatient or frustrated when you think about those who do not do things your way?

The humble person is feisty about taking their soul to task and would see these questions as opportunities to continue the lifelong transformation into Christlikeness. That attitude is a core characteristic of the humble person—a humility that seeks critique even if the person bringing the evaluation does not present the assessment correctly. Like an investigative reporter, the humble soul will figure out the bits and pieces of truth they can apply to their lives. Like a desert wanderer searching for water, they see God's hand in corrective measures because they want to change.

What about Mable?

Mable is in bondage to sin. Her two controlling sins are self-righteousness and fear of man. Mable needs a friend willing to come alongside her in a permanent, persevering, and persuasive way. Her problems are not as much about amputation (Matthew 5:29–30), though she needs to cut out some things, as they are about mortification (Romans 8:13), the long process of removing the vitality from the sins that have gripped her heart. Her restoration will not be a quick fix. She must know that this kind of friend will walk with her through the thick and thin of her junk. Her friend must be for her (Romans 8:31), a necessity for why counseling would not be the best option for Mable. Biblical counseling is an artificial context that anticipates change within that temporal construct and timeframe. Mable does not need a therapist. She needs a co-laboring friend willing to put up with her and her game-playing.

CHURCH CONSTRUCT

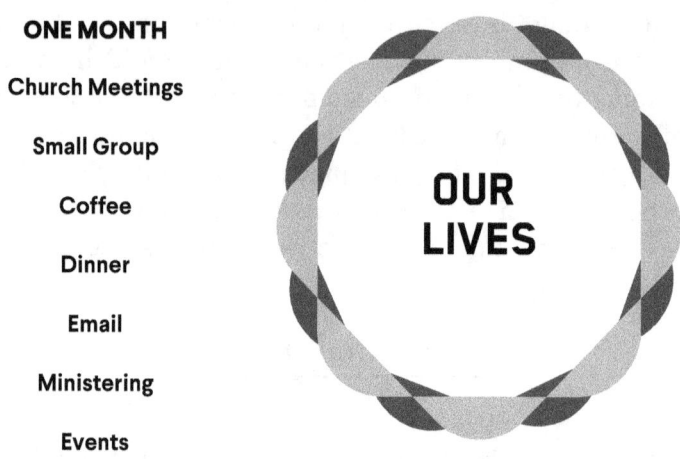

ONE MONTH

Church Meetings

Small Group

Coffee

Dinner

Email

Ministering

Events

OUR LIVES

This friend would set up multiple contexts to engage and interact with her. She needs someone to do life with her, as the graphic illustrates. Mable's sin did not sprout up in the past few months. Her sin patterns have long roots—reaching back into her childhood, and it will take much competence, compassion, courage, and continuity to walk with her through the thick weeds that have entangled her soul. As a woman with the world's worst sunburn, you cannot bring quick and decisive care to her. If you touch her, you will hurt her, but you must "touch" her. After you "hurt" her, she will "hurt" you in return, which will be a relationship cycle that you must endure. There is no way around this inevitability. The process of cooperating with the Lord in the transformation of her soul will be painstakingly complex and lengthy. More than likely, you will become frustrated with her, which is why you must heed Paul's advice.

Brothers, if anyone is caught in any transgression, you who are spiritual should restore him in a spirit of gentleness. Keep watch on yourself, lest you too be tempted. Bear one another's burdens, and so fulfill the law of Christ.

(Galatians 6:1–2)

Call to Action

The good news is that she has a local church with caring disciple-makers. They will be able to bring long-term care to her while also helping Biff to continue to mature through his issues. In time, within the context of a ready-to-disciple, loving community, this couple should receive the help they need. What about you?

1. In what ways are you like Mable? All of us are. Please explain.
2. Do you have a community of friends who speak into your life, even correcting you? Do you make it easy for them, or are they like Mable's family— always on-guard and unsure if it's safe to bring up something? Please explain.
3. Will you work through the questions I listed under self-assessment and answer them with a friend?

7

Reason to Love You

Love is a verb, an action word. It moves, always going in one direction or the other. Love will not work if it is not moving toward something. You will find it sandwiched between a subject and an object, always expecting the subject to move it toward the object. Love standing alone is a neutral concept; it cannot survive without the giver and receiver. We see this threefold cooperative requirement of love in the most famous verse in the Bible.

Love's Opportunity

> For God so loved the world, that he gave his only Son, that whoever believes in him should not perish but have eternal life.
>
> (John 3:16)

God—subject—is the lover, and we—objects—are the loved ones. This verse has brought endless joy to millions of souls as they reflect on the infinite depth and ever-broadening sweep of God's love. One of the benefits of being on the transformative end of God's love is that we can go and do likewise, looking for other potential candidates to be objects of God's redemptive love. We know the power and value of love because when the Pharisees asked Jesus about the greatest commandment, He said that out of the 600 plus laws in the Old Testament, the top two having something to do with love—to love God and others most of all.

> And he said to him, "You shall love the Lord your God with all your heart and with all your soul and with all your mind. This is the great and first commandment. And a second is like it: You shall love your neighbor as yourself. On these two commandments depend all the Law and the Prophets.
> (Matthew 22:37–40)

Self-centered Love

In the two great commandments you note the action of love; it is heading away from the givers and landing on the objects, whether God or our friends and enemies. God-centered love has a distinct directional force, and it comes from us and toward others, even if those recipients are our not-so-friends. Self-centered love is not that; it inverts itself onto the giver. The giver and the receiver of the action are one and the same. The love goes from the giver and turns 180 degrees to return to the one who sent it. In addition to this circular self-love endless loop, the self-centered lover, like a crack addict, demands even more attention, more acts of service, more words of affirmation, and more sacrifices from others. This person becomes the unfillable love cup. Self-lovers deplete and discourage their friends, eventually repelling everyone from them because nobody can carry that much water for the insatiable, selfish, thirsty soul. Eventually, these relationships die.

> There is a way that seems right for the self-centered lover, but the end of that kind of narcissistic life is the death of their relationship.
>
> (Proverbs 14:12, paraphrase)

Gospel-centered Love

Then, there is gospel-centered love with its radical, counterintuitive message, cutting against the grain of our self-esteem practitioners. Loving someone more than me does not sound right. It appears foolish and impotent, never providing what I crave (1 Corinthians 1:25). Christ modeled this kind of love when He came to earth as a human by setting aside His greatness for others (Philippians 2:5–11). Though He sacrificed so much, He understood how following the counterintuitive force and direction of gospel love would end well with Him (Hebrews 12:2). Natural humans do not do accounting like Jesus. We natively understand that if we give something away, as He did, we will have less of what we had before giving it to someone. The problem with this kind of reasoning is that God's thoughts and methods transcend ours (Isaiah 55:8–9). He challenges the natural thinker's perspectives and practices (1 Corinthians 2:14).

- Am I willing to set aside my way for a better way?
- Can I trust Christ in this matter of self-sacrificing love?
- Is it true that if I give more, I will be made whole, and those around me will not just benefit from my sacrifice, but they might find a compelling reason to do likewise?

The Fullness of Love

Give, and it will be given to you. Good measure, pressed down, shaken together, running over, will be put into your lap. For with the measure you use it will be measured back to you.

(Luke 6:38)

Some of the fullest, happiest, whole, and non-needy people that you'll ever meet are generous people who do not pine away in their victimness, always expecting others to feel sorry for them while drawing a few into their self-absorbed net of inverted love (2 Corinthians 4:16). These dried-up, sad sacks are some of the stingiest among us, always expecting and demanding while punishing anyone who refuses to meet their unmeet-able requests (Ecclesiastes 1:8, 12:1). Indeed, God-centered and self-centered love is the clashing of two mindsets.

- How would you characterize your love? Is it primarily God-centered or self-centered?
- What are a few things that hinder you from loving others like Christ, assuming there might be at least one thing?
- Perhaps another question to ask: what hinders you from loving others the way Christ has loved you?
- Will you share with a friend how God-centered love does not deplete but fills you with confidence and desire to love others more?

The Fear of Love

Typically, these questions poke at some of our hidden fears and idolatries, especially those new to self-sacrifice or those habitualized in self-centered thinking. Most self-centered lovers fear the consequences of choosing a life of giving over receiving. Often, they are guarding against losing something because their naturally trained minds teach them that receiving is better than giving. It might sound like, "If I think less about myself and more about others, will I be happy? Will I get what I crave? Will God care for me while I spend my life loving others?" The answer is a resounding, "Yes." We see this at the end of the great other-loving passage in Philippians. Notice how the Father blessed Jesus for His sacrifice.

> And being found in human form, he humbled himself by becoming obedient to the point of death, even death on a cross. Therefore God has highly exalted him and bestowed on him the name that is above every name, so that at the name of Jesus every knee should bow, in heaven and on earth and under the earth.
>
> (Philippians 2:8–10)

- Do you believe God will take care of you if you pursue Him and others most of all? Please explain.
- Do you believe that trusting God in this matter of love's direction is the best course for your life? Why?
- Is there another master tugging at your soul, enticing you to think more about yourself (Matthew 6:24)? If yes, please share more.
- What would it take to become an other-centered lover, assuming you need to change the directional flow of your love habits?

The Irony of Love

We understand the culture's twisted version of self-love, which they call self-esteem. They are the "senders and receivers" of love, but did you know that you're supposed to love yourself? Do you realize that this love is not self-centered? How sad would it be for image-bearers not to like themselves—what God created? (Genesis 1:27). Why would you not love yourself if God created you? To un-love something God made is ungodly. But you ask, "Are there dangers in loving yourself?" That's obvious. Are there dangers with anything we do? Of course, but risks should not cause a person to overreact, jumping headlong into the ditch of self-hate or self-harm. Jesus did say that we are to love our neighbor as we love ourselves. The implication is clear: we are to love ourselves. James implied a similar thing in his passage on the tongue.

> With it we bless our Lord and Father, and with it we curse people who are made in the likeness of God. From the same mouth come blessing and cursing. My brothers, these things ought not to be so.
> (James 3:9–10)

Let me push the envelope: the reason we love the gay person and the liberal-minded person is the same reason we love ourselves: because God created all of us in His image. What biblical reason would anyone have not to love an image-bearer? (I'm not speaking about loving what they do.) I act out my love for myself every day. When I have a headache, I take medication because I love myself. When I'm tired, I go to bed because I love myself. I do not deprive myself of food when I'm hungry because I love myself. The truth is that I do not hate myself, and God does not want me to go around poor-mouthing and hating myself. Self-worth (made in God's image) and self-love are different things. One of the worst manifestations of groveling, grumpy, navel-gazing self-haters among Christians is the woe is me, worm theology worldview that does not value the image-bearer. They have twisted the words of Christ to say, "Love God and others as you hate yourself," which makes no sense at all. You should love yourself because of who created you. The painting finds value in itself because of the painter. If the painter had no value, the painting would be worthless. Our Painter has inestimable worth; because of who He is, we are worth something too.

Call to Action

1. Do you know how to love yourself biblically? Will you share why you love all image-bearers, including yourself, with a friend?
2. Talk about the dangers of loving yourself. When would self-love cross the line? Has your love become self-centered? If so, why or how did it become that way, and what do you need to do to change?
3. Do you struggle with shame and guilt? Self-harm? How can someone help you overcome these problems to find satisfaction and rest as one created in God's image?
4. Describe how you can "love" a despicable person. How would that love be different from the love you have for a parent, spouse, or child, practically speaking?
5. I have asked you several questions throughout this chapter. Will you review them for self-reflection and also make them part of how you help your friends, particularly those struggling with guilt, shame, and self-harm? Their wrong focus on themselves will keep them inverted, deepening self-centered thinking until they come to the crossroad of repentance or suicide.

8

How to Feel Better

Newsflash: I have always known that something was wrong with me, but for the longest time, I did not know what it was. As I became older, I realized that it was an internal awkwardness, a sense of shame. To compensate for my soul dysfunction, I craved acceptance and approval from others. I fell prey to self-generated value, even manipulating others to like me. I connected my value as a human to the opinions of others. It would have been a good day if they had given me the proverbial thumbs up. If they gave me the thumbs down, the clouds rolled in as I slithered away in search of significance another way.

Self-generated Value

The person who longs and lives for the approval or acceptance of others while always guarding against their rejection is bowing to the gods of this world. Wanting to be wanted by someone does not have to be wrong, but we can quickly flip it on its head by permitting that desire to control us, even training us to do things we would never do if God managed our hearts. For the first twenty-five years of my life—before God regenerated me, I sought self-generated and manipulated love by pretzeling myself into whatever person I needed to become so others would accept me. I grew my hair down my back because my friends had theirs down their backs. I became a post-60s hippie. I would drink beer because my friends did. The ironic thing is that I never enjoyed beer of any kind. It's instructive of what a person will do for the acceptance of someone. I smoked weed because my friends did it. My worldview was to become what I needed to so that others would invite me into their fold. The essence of my worldview was to create the perception of value, so others would enjoy being around me.

Typically, I would find the most comfortable clique to belong to without going off the deep end, though I teetered along the edge too many times. The path of least resistance for me was to grow my hair long because I would never win friends or influence people on the field of play. I was a smallish, uncoordinated kid. Smoking weed was easier than getting good grades because it took less effort. I went with my strengths. Creating and sustaining self-worth is like a weightlifting marathon without any relief. It required more work than I could deliver. Eventually, it landed me in jail, which was one of the best things to happen to me. Our culture makes it easier than ever to have self-generated value. You can dye your hair, enhance your breasts, tuck your tummy, and even throw your food back up until you become the person you hope others find appealing. You can go the chemical route to alter your physique. You can present your most favorable self on socials, hoping to receive likes and shares. You can dive into the fantasy world of porn where the average underachiever can create a cyber universe of desperate women to fawn all over him.

Testimony of Scripture

Then there is the Word of God—the ultimate show-stopper. The testimony of Scripture digs deep into dark, despairing, and desperate hearts. In a word, the Word says that we are totally and entirely worthless! Harsh? Unkind? Image shattering? Is it damaging to one's self-esteem? What about our fragile psyches? Maybe we ought to take a look. Paul said this in Romans 3:12:

> All have turned aside; together, they have become worthless, no one does good, not even one.

Isaiah said,

> We have all become like one who is unclean, and all our righteous deeds are like a polluted garment.
>
> (Isaiah 64:6)

Paul ties his matter-of-fact declaration to our inability to achieve any merit or righteousness outside of the alien righteousness of Christ. He's talking about original and imputed sin. Having worthless righteousness and worthless worth are two different things. God made us in His image, which makes us valuable because of Him, but our fallen state makes us incapable of generating righteousness. There's more about our original and imputed badness from God's Word, but I'll not deflate you entirely, though that might not be a bad idea—or at least it helps me to become less stuck on myself when the mirror of Scripture stares me down without apology. It's just when I start to feel pretty good about myself that the Bible grabs my heart and says that I am worthless. I am the lowest of the low. I stink—from the inside out!

This worldview brought me to the crossroads of righteousness. The Bible prods me to decide if I will create my goodness so others will like me or if I will find righteousness somewhere else. Self-generated righteousness, the more technical term I have been talking about, is tiring and insatiable. There is no end to its demands, and it mandates that I must always be on guard, ever vigilant, hoping never to make the fatal mistake that would put me on the outs with the ones I expect to fill my love cup. Christ-generated righteousness is not dependent on my works because I'm resting in His good deeds on my behalf. His laborious and heroic work for me motivates me to cease striving. Jesus brings order to the chaotic craving of my soul.

Danger, My Friend

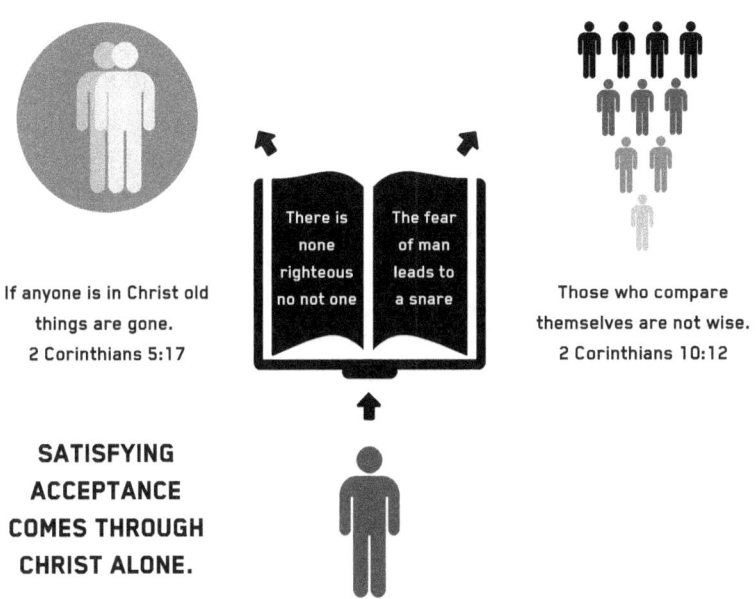

If anyone is in Christ old things are gone.
2 Corinthians 5:17

There is none righteous no not one

The fear of man leads to a snare

Those who compare themselves are not wise.
2 Corinthians 10:12

SATISFYING ACCEPTANCE COMES THROUGH CHRIST ALONE.

Be warned: There is danger ahead if you choose Jesus' work over yours. You will not be free from the temptation to conjure up your righteousness. Your pride will not let you experience uninterrupted satisfaction in Christ because you'll want to receive some acclaim. You must die daily. The devil in you—original sin—will push you to promote yourself. Your hideous desires to garner people's affection will always be crouching at the door of your heart. Fight this, my friend. Don't give in to the daily temptation to promote your value through self-generated efforts.

The person who realizes they are worthless regarding their righteousness is the individual who is ready to receive another righteousness that is far superior to any self-glorification that they could ever muster up. Practically speaking, I have to attack my pride by immersing myself in God's Word, regular praying, and a group of friends willing to carefully and lovingly speak into my life. Without the watchful eye of my wife, children, and friends, my self-righteousness will grow unchallenged. The graphic represents a sketch I have used in counseling sessions to illustrate these temptations to lean into our understanding rather than submit to God's power through His enabling grace.

The boy at the bottom is me. The people in the group at the upper right are the ones that I hope will like me. I sense I need their approval and acceptance, and I fear their rejection. Jesus is in the circle. The testimony of Scripture says that I am worthless. I have no inherent goodness; even my good stuff is rotten in the eyes of God (Isaiah 64:6). I'm a mess with no ability ever to change my condition. While I can fake out others for a season through my self-generated righteousness, it becomes vain work that leads to a wasted life. Jesus Christ is the exact opposite; He has value. He is righteous, and I want to find myself in Christ because I cannot create what He offers freely.

If you're going to feel better about yourself, you must find Christ. Not only does He have value, but He is valued—the Father loves the Son. The Father is only pleased with me when I'm in His Son. It is like someone appreciating you for the clothes you are wearing. As long as I have the righteousness of Christ clothing me, I am fully valued, treasured, loved, approved, accepted, and never rejected by the Father. My value is in Christ alone! I can't work to get it, and I can't do anything to lose it. Jesus is the treasure in this jar of clay, which can satisfy any soul (2 Corinthians 4:7). Rather than craving the uncapturable approval that too many crave from fallen people, you can fully rest in the inextinguishable righteousness of Jesus Christ. In Christ, we can cease striving for people-pleasing.

Call to Action

1. Is Christ's righteousness enough for you? Please explain.
2. What subtle ways do you get people to praise you? Humble brag? What's your trick to trick others into liking you?
3. Are you okay with others correcting you? Do you allow others to care for you, specifically when challenging you? Please explain.
4. Are you daily growing in your desire to have Christ's righteousness alone? Talk about how the gnawing internal awkwardness of shame is shrinking.
5. How are you practically allowing your friends to help you in your fight against self-righteousness? If you're not having those conversations, will you ask the Father to bring a close, trusted friend into your life so you both can benefit from the richness of these conversations?
6. Who speaks into your life? How are they helping you mature in Christ?

9

Loving Others and You

There is confusion among some believers over Christ's words about loving others as we love ourselves. The sticking point is about what loving ourselves mean. Typically, it runs along the lines of, how do you love others as you love yourself as fallen people with mixed motives? I see the ditches, with self-hate in one and self-love in the other. How can I love myself correctly and appropriately care for my fellow image-bearers? This concept of loving God and others as I love myself can be murky to a few of our brothers and sisters.

Ditch Dwellers

"Teacher, which is the great commandment in the Law?" And he said to him, "You shall love the Lord your God with all your heart and with all your soul and with all your mind. This is the great and first commandment. And a second is like it: You shall love your neighbor as yourself. On these two commandments depend all the Law and the Prophets."

(Matthew 22:36–40)

A great place to begin is by returning to the garden of Eden before transgressions when love was pure, and they did it well because there was no sin anywhere. There is nothing to unlove in a perfect world. Assuredly, Adam loved himself because you can't believe he hated himself. Imagine it. It is a challenge for post-fall people to perceive how loving yourself could be right and pure (Genesis 3:6). Pre-fall creatures could only love themselves purely because it could not be any other way. Our problem is that we live in a post-fall world, so our love for ourselves is convoluted at best and turns in on itself at worst. Our inwardly curved hearts send us into the ditches of self-hate or self-esteem. It should be apparent to anyone that we must not hate ourselves, but in a post-fallen world, there are many self-haters among us. Jesus is assuming in Matthew 22:36–40 that we already love ourselves (in the purest way that we can and should love ourselves even as a fallen creature).

Jesus could not be talking about an impure love of yourself because it would imply sin, and He would never say we should love ourselves from a sinful perspective, motive, or desire. If you're thinking rightly about God and yourself, you should not hate yourself, whether during the pre-fall with Adam and Eve or the post-fall with the rest of us. If you hate yourself, there is much heart work to get out of that ditch. Everyone understands the temptation to love ourselves the wrong way, which is why the culture has a self-esteem gospel. What would you expect God-rejectors to propagate? If you remove the Bible from your worldview, the primary thing a fallen person would be motivated to do is self-love. Without any governor, there would be no limit to how much we would love ourselves. Totally depraved and unrestricted minds know no limit to how far into the darkness they will go. Part of their curricula would say that to experience wholeness, you must love yourself more than God and others, a narcissistic type of love.

Loving the Painter

But let's say that God has regenerated the wayward soul. This person knows they must fight, always resisting any temptation to hate what God has created, including themselves. This Christian wants to cooperate with God to reverse the curse; part of that means maturing into Christlikeness, a model nobody could reasonably hate. It would be sacrilegious to hate yourself because you would hate your Creator and the new righteousness imputed to you, albeit unwittingly or passively. To hate the painting is to make a hateful commentary about the Painter. The newly minted, regenerated person shakes off this worldly way of thinking about love that drives them inward to a morbid, all-consuming, and deteriorating self-love. Of course, it's not easy for every Christian to fight this fight.

Depending on the consequences of the horrific shaping influences that have complicated a soul, like an angry parent and other demeaning authority figures, the believer will have difficulty coming to a biblio-centric way of loving themselves. As they mature, they will export their biblical love to others, always striving to live in this biblio-centric sweet spot. They might say, "I love you biblically as I love myself biblically." Because of a lack of sinless perfection, they'll always struggle with the warping shame-shaping effects of their unique Adam-ness, plus what the other mean people have put on them. Their fight will be continuous, working against over-sensitivity that tempts them to be offended and angered or always angling for the favorable opinions of others through their proactive manipulations. Without active repentance, they will not experience liberation. They will always be bound to self-love that will descend into controlling other people to ensure that they live in a carefully governed environment that steers all good opinions toward themselves. Should this happen, they must go back to the garden, realizing that God created them in the best possible image (Genesis 1:27) and that there is nothing to hate other than their sin (Romans 7:24–8:1). As they do this, they will be on guard against the tendencies that tempt them to turn the Imago Dei into a self-centered love that has less concern for others and more concern for themselves, i.e., protecting their reputation, hiding their shame, and rejecting perceived rejections.

Call to Action

1. Describe what it might be like to live in the ditch of self-hate.
2. Describe what it might be like to live in the ditch of self-love.
3. Describe what it is like to live in the middle with a biblical understanding and practice of loving yourself.
4. Why is it wrong to hate your Imago Dei?
5. Why is it wrong to hate another Imago Dei?
6. What is the balance between respecting someone's Imago Dei and disagreeing with their opinions or practices?

10

Case Study

Thank you for completing my book. I trust it has been an instructive and encouraging journey. As you wrap up, I'd like you to complete this case study. It is one of forty-eight that I have written for our Mastermind Program, our all-online, self-paced training course that teaches Christians how to disciple each other, also called biblical counseling. Anyone can take this course if it's the right season to delve into a long-form, interactive training program. You may learn more about the training at our website or drop us a note, and we will point you in the right direction. I encourage you to study this case, respond to the questions, and then share what you have learned from this book and the conclusions you have come to regarding this case study.

How Would You Counsel Mable?

Mable said during one of her counseling sessions that her dad was unstable, which typically manifested as pouting or verbal outbursts toward her and her three siblings. Mable is nineteen now but remembers in vivid detail balling up in a fetal position many nights as she listened from her bedroom to the "fights" between her dad and mom. Her mother worked full-time outside of the home. For the most part, Mable reared herself during the day while at night she lived in low-grade fear, never knowing what her dad may do next. During high school, she dated several boys and was promiscuous with most of them.

She just broke up with another boyfriend, which is why she wants to see you for counseling. From her perspective, she is suffering from low self-esteem. She has read In Search of Significance and several other self-help books that teach how her primary problem is a low view of herself, which is how she came to her conclusion. Mable became a believer two years ago but has grown very little due to her lack of connection with her local church and nobody's willingness to take her under their wing for ongoing discipleship.

Case Study Questions

1. Is her problem low self-esteem? Why did you answer the question the way that you did?
2. What is the difference (if any) between low self-esteem and low self-worth? Be clear and specific with your answer.
3. How would you counsel her? Please address the case from at least five different angles, bringing practical care to help her overcome the various issues she needs to consider and change.

About the Author

Rick Thomas launched the Life Over Coffee global training network in 2008 to bring hope and help for you and others by creating resources that spark conversations for transformation. His primary responsibilities are resource creation and leadership development, which he does through speaking, writing, podcasting, and educating. In 1990 he earned a BA in Theology and, in 1991, a BS in Education. In 1993, he received his ordination into Christian ministry, and in 2000, he graduated with an MA in Counseling from The Master's University. In 2006, he was recognized as a Fellow of the Association of Certified Biblical Counselors (ACBC).

Other Books Available from
Life Over Coffee

Boasting in Weakness
Centering Your Marriage on Christ
Communication
Complete Marriage
Don't Apologize
Exchange the Truth for a Lie
Help My Marriage Has Grown Cold
Identity Crisis
Local Church
Loving Me
Mad
Marriage Devotion We Are One
Politics and Culture
Parenting Devotion from Zero to Adulthood
Sex, Temptation, and Modesty
Storm Hurler
The Cyber Effect
The Talk
Wives Leading
You Decide

www.ingramcontent.com/pod-product-compliance
Lightning Source LLC
Chambersburg PA
CBHW071535120626
46550CB00006B/2464